AFTER THE HURRICANE

poems by

Barbara W. Sass

Finishing Line Press
Georgetown, Kentucky

AFTER THE HURRICANE

Copyright © 2018 by Barbara W. Sass
ISBN 978-1-63534-681-7 First Edition
All rights reserved under International and Pan-American Copyright Conventions. No part of this book may be reproduced in any manner whatsoever without written permission from the publisher, except in the case of brief quotations embodied in critical articles and reviews.

ACKNOWLEDGMENTS

I am grateful to Peter Campion for the generous gift of his time and encouragement, for reading my poems and helping to shape this chapbook. I also thank Sally and Beth for all things especially those computer-related. And Ethan for design of the cover.

Publisher: Leah Maines
Editor: Christen Kincaid
Cover Art: "Truro Sunset" by Barbara W. Sass
Author Photo: Sally Sass
Cover Design: Ethan Proia, contact@ethanproia.com

Printed in the USA on acid-free paper.
Order online: www.finishinglinepress.com
also available on amazon.com

Author inquiries and mail orders:
Finishing Line Press
P. O. Box 1626
Georgetown, Kentucky 40324
U. S. A.

Table of Contents

After the Hurricane 1

The Great Chain of Being 2

Spring, Maybe 3

Landscape with Figures 4

June Morning 5

Not Quite Home 6

You Would Think 7

What I Need Is 8

Sunset Encounter 9

Old Book, Small Hands 10

Dishwasher 12

Victoria's Egg 13

Cezanne and Transubstantiation 14

Experiencing Clyfford Still 15

How It Happens 16

Burn My Brushes 17

Simulcast 18

To Those Coming Upon 19

In Literal Pursit 20

Ben Knows Mushrooms 21

For Sherman: pilot, partner, muse

*Yet do thy worst, old Time: despite thy wrong,
My love shall in my verse ever live young.*
William Shakespeare

After the Hurricane—Eleuthera, 2000

Where last year rock and coral reigned,
There is now a deep parabola of sand
Stroked on one side by a tidal froth
And beset on the other by
A great downed cedar forlorn
Save for being hung with gifts
From a scavenging sea:
A blue flask caught
In a scrap of yellow net,
A red plastic shard hooked
To a length of frayed white rope,
And a ragged line of seaweed
Fringing the grounded boughs.

With the tide,
Wind and wave revisit the newborn cove,
Tear anew at the scoured hollow above,
Rearrange the still life on the shore
By stealing some things and bringing more.
I wonder at such love-making
That despoils as it adores.

The Great Chain of Being

From the hall I see you in your chair,
Eyes closed, book open on your chest,
Dozing in the pale light.
Suddenly the sun clears the clouds
And the maple tree straining at the window
Explodes into the room,
Blazing red.

These leaves you used to harvest
And stuff into huge black bags
Collected, composted, turned
Into food to grow new leaves
Which you gathered again
When blazing red.

Green leaves are fine,
But scarlet, gold and crimson
Are finer: unique, unpredictable,
Exquisitely chaotic…
Only think of the worms
In the compost growing fat on decay
To provide nourishment for rebirth.
Blessed is the new spring leaf,
But as well the beauty of the fallen.

Spring, Maybe

Most of April held back the spring
Kept the days cold and gray
Grasses matted, decayed.
A thin mauve sky
Melting into bay—
Horizon denied.
How to believe a world so dead,
A landscape so rusted
Could come alive.
Each April I need strong faith
To know the lavender will thrive,
The jagged ridge will soften
Into swelling hills, and what seems
Lost will return again as an
Immensity of green.

Landscape with Figures

I saw three nuns
In full black and white sail
Floating in the dapple of
The linden trees,
Their heads inclined together
And hands hidden in sleeves
Chatting to each other.

Another missed moment
For the Leica
Lying dumb on my desk.
So now the thing itself
And not its gray echo
Must make the memory.

In the city you are provider
Hefting a shopping bag in each hand,
Green eyes intent under a black beret.
But you've lost your keys again,
So a sudden change of plans.
And you smile as you complain.

So it is with you now,
Still transcending my lens
As you read in your chair,
Doze in the sun,
Hike on a trail, staff in hand.
Attack shrubs with huge shears,
Back-pack a child atop the dunes,
Then turn and wave, silhouetted
In the gleam of the sea.

June Morning

I have been looking through
Old papers, bank statements, and bills
Which have somehow escaped the bin.
Soon faces and places crowd in
To block out the bright spring day.
How can dry reports about profit and loss
From distant years power tears,
Then terror lest all of the past should
Disappear with the trash?
Some photos remind that once
It was a joke to prefer the picture to the man,
Because then we had both in play. But now
We have only the image, and if not mislaid
Or tossed it will soon fade away. Ageing is
Not a theme to explore while the sun
Celebrates high tide at the bay.

Not Quite Home

Each day I hasten to a place
Which is not quite home, unable
To feel whole or safe, missing traces

Of intimacy. Bed, chairs and table
Remain but the windows are blind,
The rooms hollow, walls awry, unstable.

The very air is trapped, desperate to find
That whiff of burnt toast and coffee,
Dregs of living and loving left behind.

The curtained shower is mute, emptied
Of shampoo and shaving things.
The closet, shelves bare and hanger free,

Harbors a redolence that clings,
Betraying the staleness
Of your shoes, and what lingers

Of your persistent maleness.
In half-filled drawers lie
Sweaters holding your scent, pale

Yet provocative. Also a wristwatch slyly
Keeping time with a still sweeping hand.
And wallet with credit cards highly

Leveraged. What was your plan?
Why didn't you wait? I was on my way.
You took your things, but left your wallet.
Are you okay?

You Would Think

It would be about grandchildren,
About a perfect marriage interrupted
By a husband's death. About painting,
Poetry, Rwanda, Darfur, Nine Eleven, Iraq,
Haiti, earthquakes, floods, tsunamis—
That would reduce me to tears and weak knees.
No. It's all about hydrangeas.
How they float half hidden in the leaves,
Unnaturally blue blooms that bob around,
And when I look again, freeze.
How they waited four years to please,
Knowing how much I wanted them,
Taunting me with drought and rot,
Scale, droop and wilt, and when
I gave up, this spring they gave in
And did their thing.
One June morning as I cross the lawn
A few small blue flowers glint at me.
I try not to stare not wanting to scare
Them away. But they grow more vivid
With each day, from a tentative pastel
To an outrageous boisterous royal blue.
Huge now, and sheathed in giant shrubs,
They merely tolerate the yellow coreopsis,
Are amused by the lavenders and orange daylilies.
And finally, with the power of a single
Bloom, punch a dazzling blue hole
Into a milky sky that stops the heart!
God made these blooms.
I made this poem.

What I Need Is

Someone in the next room.
It's as simple as that. The radio won't do.
Must be a live person no more than fifteen feet
Away to witness me in a consistent way.
To ask what I'm doing, what

I've done, where I'm going,
Where I've been. To make me believe
That I really exist, take up space, cast a shadow.
To convince me I am important enough
To remain alive, even healthy,

Well-fed, informed and mobile.
To remind me of friends, family, and
Of my role as Desirable Dinner Companion.
Of course a real partner would be ideal
But for now what I need is
Someone in the next room.

Sunset Encounter

This wild September sunset!
Crimson purple black
Orange slashing through.
Ebullient and morose
Rowdy and serene.
Nothing seems impossible.
And so you are at my side
Sharing my gasps of surprise,
The thundering of my heart,
Pitying my fear, my 'how?'
If I turn I know I won't see you.
That was the least to lose.
It is the voice, the touch, the listening.
Who has them now?
But for the moment you are not far,
As long as the sunset lasts.
When the color wanes and you are gone,
What remains? Merely the stars.

Old Book, Small Hands

An old book overturned on a sunny
Deck, spine battered and peeling,
Gilt letters powdering on my
White skirt. I leave it there despite

The threat of a rainy night or
Dewy morning. On second thought
I pick it up and three blue cards fall out
Filled with your scrawl…another trick

To turn my thoughts to you?
Like the faltering bedside light.
Your notes remind me of your
Small hands no bigger than mine,

Delicate and backed with fine dark hairs.
Long fingers with pale oval nails,
Their touch always cool, soft, serious.
I see them turning pages, calming

A keyboard, writing on a yellow pad
Or in the margins of a book. The same
Hands now violent with passion,
Clasping mine in a shared spasm.

Odd the things I remember. Your walk,
Your tennis strokes. The way you reached
Forward or pulled sharply back. Your
Tanned legs dark below white shorts.

Your swim suits were too short
And revealed too much but you
Neither knew nor cared. Your clothes
Sense, like your politics, unselfconscious.

Green eyes and strong brow under
A dark beret; small mouth, narrow lips
And tiny teeth. The truth is I simply
Cannot put all the parts together.

I see you from afar or as an up-close
Blur unfocused because I am alone
In the enormous strangeness of your
Being absent but not really gone.

Dishwasher

Here it is.
Inescapable
Evidence of everything
Eaten in a week.
Each item color coordinated
And nesting nicely in the
Immaculate geometry:
Four luncheon plates
Five cereal bowls
Ten coffee mugs
Eleven water glasses
Three forks, three spoons
Three champagne flutes.
The very contents of my soul.
An inventory of living alone.

See it all in the landscape
Of midnight ramblings
To drain the juice jar
In the light of the fridge,
Discard the swollen
Carton of month old milk,
Confront with bitter joy
The stainless sink bereft of pots.

O where are your frantic kitchen messes?
Your reckless sodden bathtowel rages?
I'd gladly relieve Augean Hercules,
Wash a hotel load of linen,
For an instant with you.

Victoria's Egg

In the
silence of dawn
when a daylight moon
hangs oddly in a pinkish
sky, a yellow bowl glows on a
dim counter awaiting the perfection
of not just any egg nested with eleven
others but a small blue oval, pointy at
one end and swelling voluptuously at the
other. I tap it against the edge. The bowl
fills, froths into a foaming sea. In the fiery
shallow pan an amber alpine range rises
with valleys, peaks, and plains peopled
with pepper specks. But now I crave
the sizzle as well as the sight.
To savor or to see? Which is
the mightier vice? Which
the steeper delight?

Cezanne and Transubstantiation

Have you ever known that moment
When the painting becomes the painted?
That instant when flat image slides
Into fullness and perception conspires
With desire to believe? Did it really happen?

Feel that moment of suspense and fear
When the thick red brush stroke is ridged
With green, and the fine black line emerges
As both contour and shadow.

Now both pear and apple verge
At the terrifying rim of bowl.
And you must reach for the pear
Lest it tumble to its doom…remember
Being eyed by that pearl-earringed girl
As you circled the room?

Experiencing Clyfford Still

No need to talk about peeling walls
And desolate landscapes, that is
Only the surface. Now enter this world.
Be surrounded by desire, dream and device.
By that which is painted on the heart and
Incised in the mind, that which completes
A breath, propels the brush, selects the size.
Now slip into the colors, feel their embrace.
Step over and between lines and pools of light.
How were these hues laid down?
With what brush and in what order?

Do you see beneath sheer green leaves to a bloody field?
Or through a crimson veil to a grassy plain?
Then feel the dead air of an entombed place,
Or the freezing winds of starfilled space.
Drown in blackest depths, or float in sunny
Seas. Squeeze between paint and canvas in
Overlappings everywhere. At last to emerge
Breathless, stricken, and gasping for air.

How It Happens

The painting begins as a shallow
Show of flat colored shapes. Who
Would believe such a poor thing
Could reveal a steep landscape
Of hills and sea, houses and fields?
And what a sky! All this truth from
A mere juxtaposed line and hue.
Elsewhere on white painted ground
A small black square collides with a
Great pale rectangle as a blue oval
Unites the two. Soon illusion reigns:

A young woman sits at a frame
Sewing a scene into the linen.
Through the high window sunlight
Brightens her brow, cross-hatches
A shadow behind her curving back.
Suddenly tentative forms quicken,
Deepen. Details of costume and hair
Emerge and we meet Penelope making
Images she will later delete.

Burn My Brushes

After I have seen the Vermeer, I wonder.
Will the woman in ermine and yellow silk
Remove the pearl necklace she is fingering?
Will she fold it carefully into a small silver cask,
Then smile sadly in the dim mirror, turn toward
Me, eyes lowered, and leave. Perhaps as
She passes she will search my eyes for
A few anxious, maybe desperate seconds.

After I have seen the Vermeer, I wonder.
What demon has possessed that hand,
Those eyes to coax so much reality onto
A small rectangle of stretched cloth. To catch,
Focus and diffuse sunlight with skills
Still secret in our digital world. To seal
The visible in an embrace so tight as to
Create another dimension of sight.

What to do after I have seen the Vermeer?
When I collect mind and senses from
That place of perfection, of time spreading
Out to infinity, of calm completion?
When finally I face an empty canvas and reach
For my colors, those images still intact?
Burn my brushes. Trash my palette.
Flee the studio. Go to sleep.

Simulcast

Put away those opera glasses, friend.
We have a stage so big and up-close today,
All the senses are dismayed. No more
Peering around shoulders and heads
To watch a tiny diorama acres away.
This is opera in your face, complete
With enlarged pores, tonsils, nose hairs,
Sweat and spit…only the farts deleted.
All those open-mouthed high C's
Emanate from perfect O's, from whitened
Teeth below botoxed brows. But it is
All good, it even wows as we learn
Everything and more, glean meaning
In every gesture, glance and sigh
As too many truths are revealed
Sixty feet wide and forty feet high.
Soon the curtain drops, the opera ends.
But we recall little of what precedes as
The forest is upstaged by the trees.

To Those Coming Upon

My autobiography of things, naïve yet pungent,
And like my days, collected over the years. Now
To be inventoried and marked to stay or to send away.

I don't mean those things worthy of compiling
Against the future like books, letters, recipes,
Tax receipts, mortgage loans, deposit box keys.

No. I mean a hundred bundled paperclips,
Scores of feathers gathered by length and hue,
Treasures found on beach and nature trips:

Odd stones great and small, some rough, some fine.
Some set as sentry or bookends. Some to be ceaselessly
Stroked, reset, turned over and shined. And the owls:

Carved, painted, molded, of metal and clay,
Some menacing or somnolent, some gay.
Perhaps the baskets in the dozens might puzzle

Or dismay, amassed not for what and how
They carry but for their grace. To caress and
Inhale the straw, fiber, cane, and to be placed

For color and shape. Now piled together on shelves
Or thrown into corners, they play their native
Market games for our mirthless urban selves.

In Literal Pursuit

I am in pursuit of retreating nouns,
Of names once known for places, things.
Ideas still cling, but the words
For whom, what, where are gone.
Fleeing they can be regained
But only to escape again.

It is a death-struggle to wrest them,
My eyes burning and heart racing,
From their hellish hiding places.
For they are my children,
My friends, my work,
Merely my life.

I know the place, the thing, the smell.
I can see it, feel it, taste it,
Yet the word won't spell.
Only half, one syllable or two,
As the letters fade from view. Yet I know
If the chase grows desperate, just let it go.
Errant words will wander home
Often when left alone.

Ben Knows Mushrooms

We are all together in Truro
On a wet late September afternoon.
It is a mushroom gatherer's dream.
The odd pale clumps are everywhere.
Neither flowers nor fruits they gleam
In the mist. Idly I ask how to know
Which to trust and which to fear?
It is Ben who knows
Which color is good,
Which underside bad.

After a while he tells about a boy
Hiding in the Polish woods
For long lonely months
Who learns about mushrooms
And other things from the peasants.
But only a few are friends.
"And so you learn," he says,
"And you remember."

Although a native New Yorker, **Barbara Sass** has been living in the Boston area and in Truro, Cape Cod since 1960. As printmaker and poet, she has been engaged with verbal as well as visual images for much of her life. In her poetry, Barbara uses both free and formal verse, especially when traditional forms can organize, clarify and enhance meaning. Many of her poems deal with an intense response to the process and the substance of painting, and directly reflect her studio experience, as well as deep immersion in art history and criticism. Delving into a painting, she lays bare process and premise via memorable verse and image. With an MA in art history and in arts education, she served as a long-time docent at The Harvard Art Museums in Cambridge, MA. She is widowed, has two daughters and three grandchildren.

www.ingramcontent.com/pod-product-compliance
Lightning Source LLC
LaVergne TN
LVHW041521070426
835507LV00012B/1728